Famous Myths and Legends of the World

Myths and Legends of
CENTRAL AND SOUTH AMERICA

WORLD
BOOK

a Scott Fetzer company
Chicago
www.worldbook.com

World Book, Inc.
180 North LaSalle Street
Suite 900
Chicago, Illinois 60601
USA

For information about other World Book publications, visit
our website at **www.worldbook.com** or call **1-800-967-5325**.

Library of Congress Cataloging-in-Publication Data

Myths and legends of Central and South America.
     pages cm. -- (Famous myths and legends of the world)
   Summary: "Myths and legends from Central and South
America. Features include information about the history and
culture behind the myths, pronunciations, lists of deities,
word glossary, further information, and index"-- Provided by
publisher.
   Includes index.
   ISBN 978-0-7166-2628-2
   1. Aztec mythology--Juvenile literature. 2. Maya
mythology--Juvenile literature. 3. Folklore--Central America--
Juvenile literature. 4. Inca mythology--Juvenile literature.
5. Indian mythology--South America--Juvenile literature.
6. Folklore--South America--Juvenile literature. 7. Central
America--Folklore--Juvenile literature. 8. South America--
Folklore--Juvenile literature. I. World Book, Inc. II. Series:
Famous myths and legends of the world.
F1219.76.R45C76 2015
398.20972--dc23
                                     2015014761

Set ISBN: 978-0-7166-2625-1
E-book ISBN: 978-0-7166-2640-4 (EPUB3)

Printed in China by PrintWORKS Global Services,
Shenzhen, Guangdong
2nd printing May 2016

Writer: Anita Croy

Staff for World Book, Inc.
Executive Committee
President: Jim O'Rourke
Vice President and Editor in Chief: Paul A. Kobasa
Vice President, Finance: Donald D. Keller
Vice President, Marketing: Jean Lin
Director, International Sales: Kristin Norell
Director, Licensing Sales: Edward Field
Director, Human Resources: Bev Ecker

Editorial
Manager, Annuals/Series Nonfiction: Christine Sullivan
Managing Editor, Annuals/Series Nonfiction:
     Barbara Mayes
Administrative Assistant: Ethel Matthews
Manager, Indexing Services: David Pofelski
Manager, Contracts & Compliance
     (Rights & Permissions): Loranne K. Shields

Manufacturing/Production
Manufacturing Manager: Sandra Johnson
Production/Technology Manager: Anne Fritzinger
Proofreader: Nathalie Strassheim

Graphics and Design
Senior Art Director: Tom Evans
Coordinator, Design Development and Production:
     Brenda Tropinski
Senior Designers: Matthew Carrington,
     Isaiah W. Sheppard, Jr.
Media Researcher: Jeff Heimsath
Manager, Cartographic Services: Wayne K. Pichler
Senior Cartographer: John M. Rejba

Staff for Brown Bear Books Ltd
Managing Editor: Tim Cooke
Editorial Director: Lindsey Lowe
Children's Publisher: Anne O'Daly
Design Manager: Keith Davis
Designer: Mike Davis
Picture Manager: Sophie Mortimer

Picture credits
t=top, c=center, b=bottom, l=left, r=right
4-5, Shutterstock; 6, WORLD BOOK map; 7-13, Alamy; 13b, Thinkstock; 14, Thinkstock; 14-17, WORLD BOOK illustration;
18-19, Shutterstock; 19t, Alamy; 20-21, Thinkstock; 22-23, Shutterstock; 24t, Dreamstime; 24-25b, Shutterstock; 25l, Alamy;
25r, Alamy; 26-28, Shutterstock; 30l, Shutterstock; 30br, Alamy; 30-31b, Shutterstock; 31b, Alamy; 32-33, Alamy; 34-35,
Shutterstock; 36t, Corbis; 36b, Alamy; 37t, Alamy; 37b, Shutterstock; 38-39, Shutterstock; 40t, Alamy; 40b, Thinkstock;
41tl, Alamy; 41b, SuperStock; 42-43, Alamy; 44-45b, Thinkstock; 44-45t, Shutterstock; 45tr, Alamy; 45b, Corbis;
46-49t, Shutterstock; 48-51, Thinkstock; 50-51, Thinkstock; 52l, ImageBroker/Alamy; 52-53t, Alamy; 53br, Thinkstock;
54-55t, Alamy; 56-57, Dreamstime; 58, Shutterstock; 59t, Thinkstock; 59b, Corbis; back cover, Shutterstock.

CONTENTS

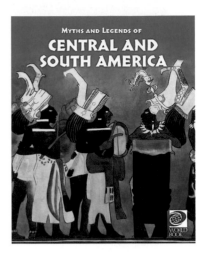

Maya musicians play drums in a reconstructed detail of a mural dating from A.D. 790, found at Bonampak, an ancient Maya archeological site in what is now the Mexican state of Chiapas.

De Agostini Picture Library/
G. Dagli Orti/Bridgeman Images

Note to Readers:

Phonetic pronunciations have been inserted into the myths and legends in this volume to make reading the stories easier and to give the reader some of the flavor of the Central and South American cultures the stories represent. See page 64 for a pronunciation key.

The myths and legends retold in this volume are written in a creative way to provide an engaging reading experience and approximate the artistry of the originals. Many of these stories were not written down but were recited by storytellers from generation to generation. Even when some of the stories came to be written down they likely did not feature phonetic pronunciations for challenging names and words! We hope the inclusion of this material will improve rather than distract from your experience of the stories.

Some of the figures mentioned in the myths and legends in this volume are described on page 60 in the section "Deities of Central and South America." In addition, some unusual words in the text are defined in the Glossary on page 62.

INTRODUCTION

Since the earliest times, people have told stories to try to explain the world in which they lived. These stories are known as myths. Myths try to answer these kinds of questions: How was the world created? Who were the first people? Where did the animals come from? Why does the sun rise and set? Why is the land devastated by storms or drought? Today, people often rely on science to answer many of these questions. But in earlier times—and in some parts of the world today—people explained natural events using stories about gods, goddesses, spirits of nature, and heroes.

Myths are different from folk tales and legends. Folk tales are fictional stories about animals or human beings. Most of these tales are not set in any particular time or place, and they begin and end in a certain way. For example, many English folk tales begin with the phrase "Once upon a time" and end with "They lived happily ever after." Legends are set in the real world, in the present or the historical past. Legends distort the truth, but they are usually based on real people or events.

The World of Vucub Caquix, page 18

Myths, in contrast, typically tell of events that have taken place in the remote past. Unlike legends, myths have also played—and often continue to play—an important role in a society's religious life. Although legends may have religious themes, most are not religious in nature. The people of a society may tell folk tales and legends for amusement, without believing them. But they usually consider their myths sacred and completely true.

Most myths concern divinities, or divine beings. These divinities have powers far greater than those of any human being. At the same time, however, many gods, goddesses, and heroes of mythology have human characteristics. They are guided by such emotions as love and jealousy, and they may experience birth and death. A number of mythological figures even look like human beings. In many cases, the human qualities of the divinities reflect a society's ideals. Good gods and goddesses have the qualities a society admires, and evil ones have the qualities it dislikes. In myths, the actions of these divinities influence the world of humans for better or for worse.

The World of the Inca, page 31

Myths can sometimes seem very strange. They sometimes seem to take place in a world that is both like our world and unlike it. Time can go backward and forward, so it is sometimes difficult to tell in what order events happen. People may be dead and alive at the same time.

Myths were originally passed down from generation to generation by word of mouth. Partly for this reason, there are often different versions of the same story.

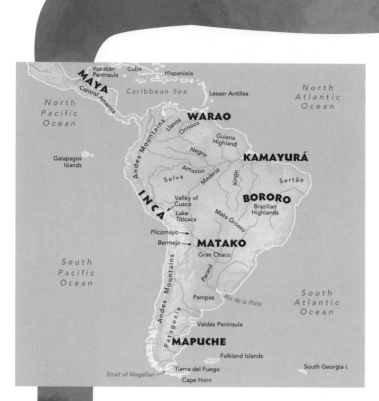

Powerful empires grew in Mexico, Central America, and farther south into the Andes Mountains of South America.

In early times, every society developed its own myths, though many myths across cultures share similar themes, such as the battle between good and evil. The myths of a society generally reflect the landscape, climate, and society in which the storytellers lived.

Myths of Central and South America

People arrived in South America as early as 30,000 years ago. By 12,500 years ago, they had spread to the lowland forests of Central America and the Andes Mountains, and from the heart of the vast Amazon rain forest to the grassy plains and wetlands of southern South America. These peoples saw the world in different ways, but they all shared a belief that different gods, goddesses, and spirits influenced their lives.

To obtain the help of the gods, the Maya—who lived in what are the present-day countires of Mexico, Guatemala, and Honduras—fasted, prayed, offered sacrifices, and held many religious ceremonies. The Maya practiced some human sacrifice, such as throwing victims into deep wells or killing them at the funerals of great leaders.

Farther south, in modern-day Peru, native civilizations flourished along the Pacific Coast long before the Inca built a powerful empire with its capital in the Andes. Sacrifices and offerings—of crops, animals, and sometimes people—were important in Inca religious ceremonies. Like other American peoples, the Inca revered the jaguar, a powerful hunter.

Many of the peoples of the rain forest continue to tell the old myths today. Some of these peoples have had little contact with the modern world. For them, myths remain part of their religious ceremonies. These stories tell people about their distant history and why their society is structured in the way it is. They show people how to behave in the world and find their way. As teaching tools, myths help to prepare children for their lives as adults.

By studying myths, we can learn how different societies have answered basic questions about the world and the individual's place in it. We can learn how a people developed a particular social system with its many customs and ways of life. By examining myths, we can better understand the feelings and values that bind members of society into one group. We can compare the myths of various cultures to discover how these cultures differ and how they resemble one another. We can also study myths to try to understand why people behave as they do.

The World of the Heavenly Twins, page 12

7

The
HEAVENLY

The Maya told this myth about the time before humans existed to explain why life was a constant battle between such opposites as good and evil.

Hunhun-Ahpu (hoon-hoon-ah-poo) and Vukub-Ahpu (voo-koob-ah-poo) were twin brothers who loved to play the ball game known as tlachtli (tlahk tlee). The brothers spent so much time playing tlachtli that they became the best players in the world.

The twins' success made the Twelve Lords of the underworld kingdom of Xibalba (shee-BALH-bah) extremely envious. The Lords believed that they were easily the best players of

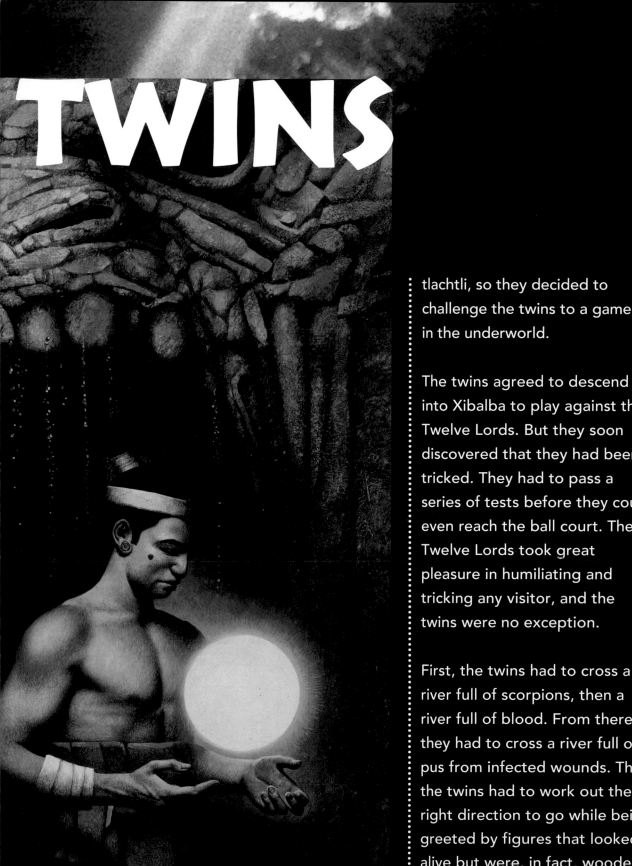

TWINS

tlachtli, so they decided to challenge the twins to a game in the underworld.

The twins agreed to descend into Xibalba to play against the Twelve Lords. But they soon discovered that they had been tricked. They had to pass a series of tests before they could even reach the ball court. The Twelve Lords took great pleasure in humiliating and tricking any visitor, and the twins were no exception.

First, the twins had to cross a river full of scorpions, then a river full of blood. From there, they had to cross a river full of pus from infected wounds. Then the twins had to work out the right direction to go while being greeted by figures that looked alive but were, in fact, wooden.

Unfortunately, the twins failed the test and did not make it to the ball court. The Lords, who were excited that the twins had failed, demanded they be put to death. The twins, who were brave and noble, agreed and were killed. The twins' bodies were buried, but the Twelve Lords hung Hunhun-Ahpu's head in a tree as a trophy. Although the tree had never borne any fruit before, the next day its branches were laden with fruit. The Twelve Lords forbade anyone from touching the tree. But one day a very curious young girl named Xquiq (shah-keek) could not resist trying one of the fruits. As she stretched out her hand, the head of Hunhun-Ahpu spat on her palm and spoke to her. "Quick," it said. "Go back to the Upperworld, where you will give birth to my sons." Terrified, the girl fled, with the Twelve Lords hot on her heels.

After Xquiq escaped to the Upperworld, she gave birth to twin boys, whom she named Hunahpu (hoon-ah-POO) and Xbalanque (shaw-BAHL-ahn-kay). The twins were brave, clever, and strong and became excellent players of the ball game.

Remembering how they had defeated the twins' father and uncle, the Twelve Lords of Xibalba now challenged the young twins to a ball game. However, this time, the twins realized that the Lords were going to trick them, so they were prepared. They managed to overcome every obstacle and challenge the Lords threw at them and finally arrived at the ball court.

At last the ball game could take place. The young twins defeated the Twelve Lords, but the Lords refused to accept defeat. After the game, they forced the twins to face even more challenges. This time the twins set their own trap. They pretended they had been defeated and allowed the gods to burn them on a funeral pyre and scatter their ashes far and

wide. But five days later, the twins reappeared as two strange figures——half-men, half-fish—that the lords did not recognize. The newcomers told the Lords that they could perform a remarkable trick—they could burn animals and then bring them back to life.

The Lords were so impressed they asked the strange figures to burn them as well. The twins were happy to oblige. As flames engulfed the Twelve Lords, the brothers threw off their disguises and told the evil Lords they would not remake them. Then they brought their father back to life. As the corn god, Hunhun-Ahpu now feeds the world. Hunahpu and Xbalanque then rose to heaven, where one became the sun and the other the planet Venus.

The World of
THE HEAVENLY TWINS

The Maya lived in what are now present-day Guatemala, southeastern Mexico, and Honduras. They were not a single empire like the Aztec of Mexico or the Inca of Peru. Instead, the Maya lived in a number of city-states, each of which had its own version of the Mayan language. The cities sometimes fought with one another but sometimes traded together. By about A.D. 900, the Maya had largely abandoned the Guatemalan lowlands and moved to areas to the north and south, including Yucatán (yoo kuh TAN) of Mexico and the highlands of southern Guatemala. In those areas, they continued to prosper until Spain conquered almost all of the Maya in the mid-1500's. Today, descendants of the Maya live in Mexico and Central America. They speak Maya languages and carry on some religious customs of their ancestors.

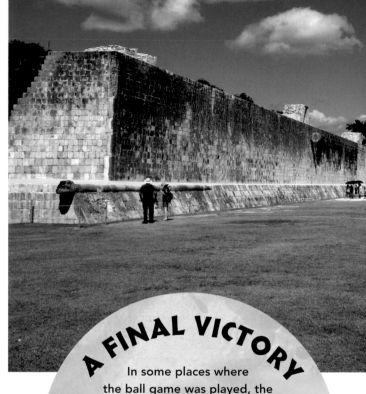

A FINAL VICTORY

In some places where the ball game was played, the losers of a game were killed as sacrifices to the gods. But at other times or in other places, it might be the captain of the winning team who was killed. The Maya believed it was a great honor to be sacrificed to the gods in this way. They believed that the victim would go straight to the Maya heaven.

A reclining figure called a chocmool looks out from the Temple of the Warriors at Chichén Itzá (chee CHEHN eet SAH). Offerings to the gods were placed in the bowl on the statue's stomach.

The Great Ball Court at Chichén Itzá (left), in what is now Mexico, was one of the largest in the Maya world. In some ball courts, players scored by touching carved stone markers, such as one showing a priest making an offering (above).

The ball game played throughout most of Central America and Mexico had a number of different names. It was most often known as tlachtli (tlahk tlee).

Although some people played the game for fun, tlachtli was not only a sport. It was also a spiritual and religious experience in which the ball may have been a symbol of the sun. The aim of the game was to pass a leather ball through a high hoop—or touch the ball to a stone marker—placed high on the wall of the ball court. But players could not use their hands during the game. They moved the ball with their knees, hips, and elbows.

VUCUB

CAQUIX

and the Hero Twins

The Maya told this myth to explain the challenges their gods had faced to make the world safe for their people.

Long ago, there lived on Earth an arrogant bird god named Vucub Caquix (voo KOOB kay KEESH). This gigantic god was the lord of the underworld, which was called Xibalba (shee-BALH-bah). Vucub Caquix was so arrogant he liked to pretend that he was the sun, moon, and light, all rolled into one. His two sons, Zipacna (zip ak NAH) and Cabraca, were no better. They made Earth shake as they burrowed under the mountains, and they refused to honor the creators who made them.

Hunahpu (hoon ah POO) and Xbalanque (shaw BAHL ahn kay), the Hero Twins, were very offended by Vucub Caquix's behavior and the lack of respect he showed the creators. They decided to wage a war against him and to destroy him. They knew that Vucub Caquix was fond of the fruit of a certain tree. So one day, they waited by the tree for him to turn up to get his daily fruit. As the bird god appeared, the twins fired a dart from a blowpipe and wounded him. But Vucub Caquix could not be beaten so easily. He fought with the twins. And in the fight, he pulled off one of Hunahpu's arms, which the bird god carried off.

Hunahpu had to get his arm back. The Hero Twins knew that the bird god's mighty strength came from his teeth, so they devised a cunning plan to take them. They disguised themselves as tooth doctors and set out to find the bird god. They tricked Vucub Caquix into letting them look in his mouth. Then they pulled out all his teeth and replaced them with sharp kernels of white corn. They also gouged out his eyes. Now that Vucub Caquix was toothless and blind, he could not stop the twins from making off with Hunahpu's severed arm, which Hunahpu easily reattached to his body.

Vucub Caquix was powerless. With his corn false teeth, he no longer even looked like a lord. Before long, he became weak and died.

But his two sons, Zipacna and Cabraca, still misbehaved. They were now determined to avenge their father's misfortune and defeat the Hero Twins. At night, Zipacna held up the mountains. That is why he was often called "creator of mountains." During the day, he hunted for fresh fish and crabs.

One day, Zipacna came across 400 men who were trying to carry a huge log to prop up the roof of a gigantic house they were building. Zipacna was so strong that he was able to carry the log all by himself and offered to help.

Unbeknownst to Zipacna, however, the men were allies of the Hero Twins, and they had come up with a plan to destroy the twins' enemies.

The men waited until Zipacna had put the huge log in place. Then they persuaded him to get into a deep pit they had dug as a trap. Once he was in the pit, they began to cover him with soil to bury him. Zipacna realized what the men were doing, so he pretended to be dead. The men, believing that they had killed him, went off to their new house to celebrate. After a while, Zipacna climbed out of the pit. He crept over to the house and pulled it down, killing all the men inside. As they died, the men were transformed into stars and rose into the sky.

When the Hero Twins found out what had happened, they decided they had to kill Zipacna themselves. They made a large crab from clay, then used the crab to lure Zipacna into a cave in a mountain with the promise of a delicious meal. Just as he was about to dig into the crab, the mountain fell on top of him and killed him.

Next the twins turned their attention to the other brother, Cabraca. He loved to hunt, so the twins invited him to go hunting with them. They hunted for birds, which were Cabraca's favorite food. When they stopped for a break, the twins offered Cabraca a bird as a snack. He gobbled it up, saying how delicious it was. He did not notice that the twins had covered the bird with soil that was deadly poisonous. After just a few bites, he fell dead.

With the death of Vucub Caquix and his arrogant sons, Zipacna and Cabraca, the Hero Twins had rid Earth of evil. It was now safe for the creators to bring the Maya into the world.

17

LEARNING ABOUT MAYA MYTHS

Modern scholars have learned about Maya beliefs and myths mainly from the *hieroglyphic* (picture) writing on walls, doorways, and *stelae* (carved-stone monuments) of the many Maya temples that have survived. Another important source of information is the sacred book of the Maya, the *Popol Vuh.* Written in Quiché (keesh), a language from the highlands of Guatemala, its name means *The Collection of Written Leaves.* It describes the creation of the Quiché people of Guatemala and contains myths, including that of the Heavenly Twins. Only a few books from the ancient Maya have survived. They contain astronomical tables, information about religious ceremonies, and calendars that show lucky days for such activities as farming and hunting.

Towering limestone pyramids topped with temples dot the ruins of Tikal in modern-day Guatemala. At its height in the A.D. 600's and 700's, Tikal was one of the largest cities of the Maya civilization.

BIRDS IN MYTH

The Maya imagined Vucub Caquix (voo KOOB kay KEESH) as a bird god who pretended to be the sun and the moon. Other birds occur in the myths of many peoples around the world. In North America, many peoples told stories about Raven, a trickster god who sometimes helped people but who sometimes caused mischief. According to one ancient Egyptian myth, the first god was the long-legged Benu bird, which waded in the waters when the world was first created.

A carving of what appears to be the bird-god Vucub Caquix, with a sharp beak and wide, threatening wings, appears on a clay bowl.

The Maya developed mathematics and astronomy. They used a mathematical system based on the number 20, instead of 10 as in the decimal system. A dot represented the number one, a bar represented five, and special symbols represented zero. The Maya were among the first people to use symbols for the idea of zero. Maya priests observed the positions of the sun, moon, and stars. They made tables predicting eclipses and describing the orbit of the planet Venus.

Maya priests also used mathematics and astronomy to develop two kinds of calendars. One was a sacred almanac of 260 days. The other calendar had 365 days and was based on the orbit of Earth around the sun.

← Maya writing consisted of many symbols, which represented combinations of sounds or entire ideas.

A terracotta Maya figurine, created between A.D. 600 and 900, shows an official writing in a book.

The Creation of the
CORN PEOPLE

The Maya told this myth to explain the origins of humans. The story also reminded people of the gratitude they owed to the gods and how important it was to honor them in the correct way.

When the world began, there was nothing apart from sky and sea. So the god Heart-of-the-Sky-and-Earth, who was also called Huracán (hoo rah KAHN), called on Earth to form and it did. Then the god, who had bolts of lightning shooting from his head, created land. He filled the land with all kinds of animals, large and small, and told them where and how to live. Huracán wanted the animals to obey him and to praise him and the other gods. But because the animals were animals, they could not speak—they just made squawking noises. Huracán decided they were not suitable creatures to rule Earth. For this reason, Huracán did not yet make the sun rise on his creation.

Huracán decided to create a creature that could rule over the animals and praise the gods properly. He decided he would make a man. But what should he make a man out of? First he decided to use clay, because it was easy to find in the ground. But the clay man was hopeless; he could speak, but what he said made no sense. When he got wet, his body, which was weak to begin with, began to dissolve and disintegrate. The

god gave up. He broke his creation
apart and started all over again.

The next man was made out of wood.
The wooden man could speak, but he
was very rude. He didn't have any
feelings. Huracán made more wooden
men, but he was in for a shock. The
wooden men refused to pray to any god,
and they were horrible to the animals. It
was clear that the wooden men were
unsuitable, so Huracán decided to start
again. He sent a huge flood to wash the
wooden men away. As the waters rose,
the wooden men drowned.

Huracán realized that he was not making much progress on his own, so he called on other gods to help him create a man. The gods had a discussion. "What's the greatest of all the plants?" they asked. Well, the answer was obvious. It was corn. So the gods gathered the finest ears of yellow, white, red, and black corn and ground them into cornmeal. They mixed half the meal with water and shaped the paste into four men. They boiled the other half of the meal into a rich broth, which they fed to the four men.

The men the gods created were wise and noble. They were grateful to Huracán and thanked him for creating them. But Huracán was still not happy.

He could see that the men were too wise. He feared that they might grow too powerful and that one day they might challenge the gods. So he breathed a veil over their eyes that would limit their wisdom. From then on, the men could no longer see the spiritual world. They were aware only of the physical world that was right in front of them.

Huracán sent the men to sleep. While they slept, he created four women to act as companions for them. When the corn men awoke, they had no idea what had happened, but they were delighted to meet their new female companions. For the first time, the sun rose, and the four corn men and four corn women watched the sunrise together.

The World of **HURACÁN**

Ah Mun (ah muhn), who was also known as Yum Kaax (yoom KAHSH), was the Maya corn god and the god of agriculture. He was a major god, as he reflected how important farming was to the Maya. Ah Mun was always shown as a young god, to symbolize growth and health, and was often portrayed with ears of corn sticking out of his headdress. The Maya prayed to Ah Mun for plentiful harvests and offered sacrifices to him.

Archeologists believe that the Maya used wooden plates to shape their babies' skulls so that their heads would become elongated, like an ear of corn.

A clay mask painted green depicts the Maya corn god.

THE IMPORTANCE OF CORN

It is not surprising that humans were made from corn in the Maya creation myth. The Maya were farmers whose chief crop was corn (maize). They used corn to make tortillas and tamales, which were part of every meal, and *atole* (ah TOH lay), a hot drink. Corn was worshiped as a nutritious food supply that was easy to grow and store. The Maya grew corn in fields as well as in valleys and on steep hillsides. Corn allowed the Maya to settle into communities and formed the basis of their civilization.

THE WORLD TREE

The Maya believed in a World Tree (Wakah-chan [wah kah chahn] "raised-up sky") that joined the Overworld, Middleworld, and Underworld into a cosmic whole. This green tree is at the center of the world. Dead souls travel along its trunk to the Underworld. Its roots reach as far as the Underworld, and its top reaches the heavens. In the Middleworld are four special trees, each of which grows in one direction and is a different color. North is white; south is yellow; east is red; and west is black. The birds and animals living in each of those directions are that same color. The four colors are also the colors of the corn kernels used to make the first humans.

Maya men and women had clearly defined roles in society. Men were warriors (left) and hunted for food. Women performed all of the tasks within the home, including preparing and cooking food, raising children, and weaving. They wove textiles on a loom they strapped around their back to keep the fibers taut (below). Men and women worked together in the fields when it was time to plant or harvest the crops. Although men and women had specific jobs, women could be powerful in Maya society. Noblewomen influenced the Maya rulers and joined their husbands in making sacrifices to the gods.

PACHACAMAC
Sends the Inca

The Inca told a number of myths to explain how their state had been founded at Cuzco in the valleys of the Andes. This story echoes historical events, when the early Inca fought and defeated their neighbors to take control of the Valley of Cuzco.

At the beginning of the world, Pachacamac (pah chuh KAH mahk), the sun, rose from Lake Titicaca (tee tee KAH kah). Pachacamac was so bright he outshone anything else in the sky. But the night sky was empty, so Pachacamac made the stars, the planets, and the moon. The beautiful moon, Pachamama (pak-uh-ma-ma), became his wife, and together they ruled the heavens and Earth.

Pachacamac made the first people out of stone that he took from an enormous mountain rock. But these humans were pitiful. They lived like animals with no housing or clothing, eating human flesh, wild plants, and the roots of trees.

Pachacamac took pity on his creations and decided to send his son, Manco Capac (MAHN koh KAH pahk), and his daughter, Mama Ocllo (MAH mah oh KLOH), to Earth to help them. The son was to teach the people how to worship the sun, build houses, and plow and sow crops. The daughter would teach the women how to weave cloth and prepare food.

Pachacamac sent his two children down to Lake Titicaca and ordered them to

travel in any direction they chose.
Wherever they stopped to sleep, he
instructed them to push a rod made of
gold into the ground. The rod, which
measured the length of a man's arm and
was two fingers thick, was a sacred sign
from Pachacamac. When the son and his
sister-wife reached a place where the
rod disappeared into the ground with a
single thrust, they were to found a city.
The son would become the first Inca
king and have his royal court there.

The two children emerged from the
waters of Lake Titicaca and traveled
north. Whenever they stopped, they

pushed the golden rod into the ground.
But it would not disappear. Eventually,
the brother and his sister-wife came to
the Valley of Cuzco (KOOS koh), which
was then a wild land. They stopped first
at a hill called Rainbow and pushed the
golden rod into the ground. It was
swallowed up! Manco Capac said to
his sister-wife, "This is the spot where
our Father the Sun said we should build
our city."

Now they spread out to gather people
for the new city. Manco Capac went
north, and his sister-wife went south.
As they traveled through the

wilderness, they told the men and women they met how their Father the Sun had sent them to Earth to be their rulers and benefactors. For their part, the people could not believe the beautiful robes and gold jewelry the Inca and his sister-wife wore.

The people could see that they were the children of the Sun and believed their new rulers were there to help them live in towns and to feed them so they would not be hungry again. For that reason, the people worshiped the Inca and his sister-wife.

People left their small villages and followed Manco Capac and his sister-wife back to the Valley of Cuzco.

Soon, followers from all over the region came to live there. The Inca ordered some of the people to provide food so that no one was hungry. Then he gave them a model of a house and told them to make copies of it. This was how the city of Cuzco came to be built.

The city was divided into two halves—Upper and Lower Cuzco. Those who had been summoned by the Inca lived in the upper half, and those who had been summoned by his sister-wife lived in the lower half. From then on, all Inca cities were divided into two equal halves that represented male and female forces. When the city was built, the Inca showed the men their jobs, which were to till the land and sow corn, quinoa (KEE no ah), and vegetables. They learned how to irrigate their land so the crops had a supply of water. Manco Capac's sister-wife showed the women how to spin cotton and wool and how to weave to make clothes for everyone.

The people were so happy that they traveled around the mountains to spread the good news about the Sun's children and to show other people the benefits the Inca and his sister-wife had brought to them. These people, in turn, were so impressed that they also came to Cuzco to serve the children of the Sun. In just a few years, so many people had joined that the Inca was able to form his own army to defend his people and to extend his empire. This is the story of the first Inca, Manco Capac, and his sister-wife, Mama Ocllo, the children of the Sun and the Moon.

The World of THE INCA

The Inca ruled one of the largest and richest empires in the Americas. The Inca empire emerged in the early A.D. 1400's and occupied a vast region centered around the capital of Cuzco, in southern Peru. The empire extended over 2,500 miles (4,020 kilometers) along the western coast and mountains of South America. It included parts of present-day Colombia, Ecuador, Peru, Bolivia, Chile, and Argentina. The Inca empire was conquered by Spanish forces in 1532.

PERU'S ANDEAN LANDSCAPE

The Inca city of Machu Picchu (MAH choo PEEK choo) (right) was built on a high ridge in a heavily forested part of the Andes Mountains. It probably served as a royal estate. Scholars think Machu Picchu was abandoned shortly after the Spaniards began their conquest of the Inca. For the Inca, the landscape was sacred—any part of nature was considered a *huaca* (sacred place).

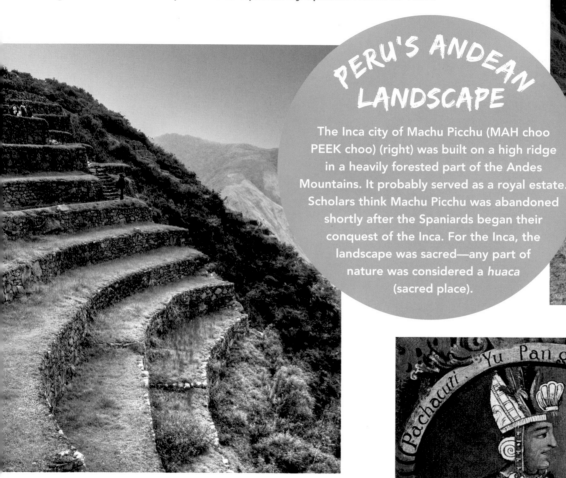

The Inca learned how to farm the steep mountain terraces, growing potatoes that could be preserved for the winter months.

Pachacuti founded the Inca empire in about 1438. He rebuilt Cuzco as the empire's magnificent capital. He also built Machu Picchu in about 1450.

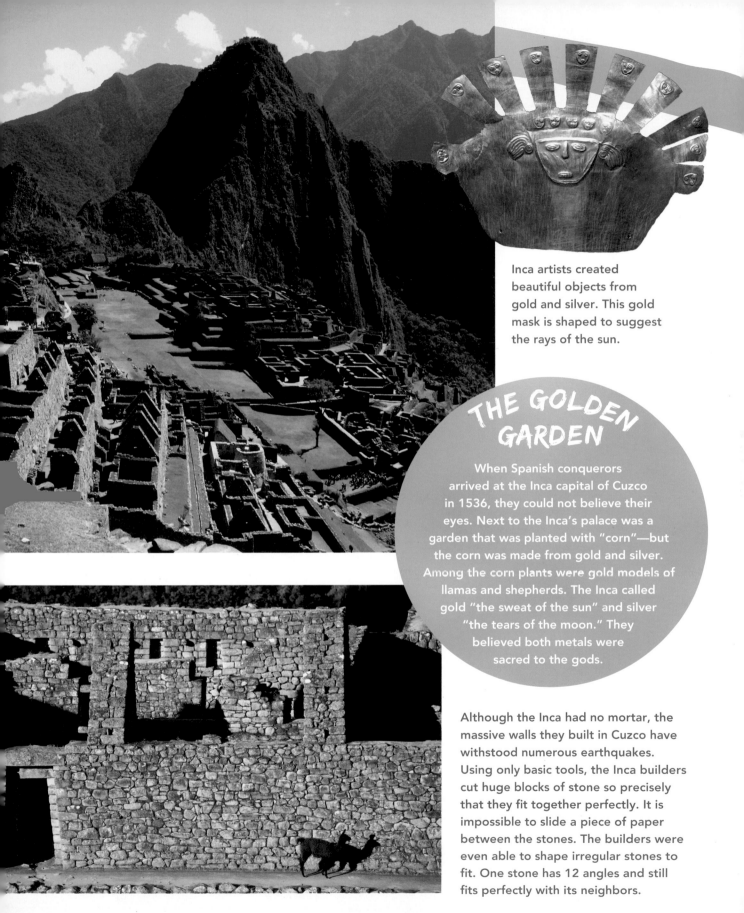

Inca artists created beautiful objects from gold and silver. This gold mask is shaped to suggest the rays of the sun.

THE GOLDEN GARDEN

When Spanish conquerors arrived at the Inca capital of Cuzco in 1536, they could not believe their eyes. Next to the Inca's palace was a garden that was planted with "corn"—but the corn was made from gold and silver. Among the corn plants were gold models of llamas and shepherds. The Inca called gold "the sweat of the sun" and silver "the tears of the moon." They believed both metals were sacred to the gods.

Although the Inca had no mortar, the massive walls they built in Cuzco have withstood numerous earthquakes. Using only basic tools, the Inca builders cut huge blocks of stone so precisely that they fit together perfectly. It is impossible to slide a piece of paper between the stones. The builders were even able to shape irregular stones to fit. One stone has 12 angles and still fits perfectly with its neighbors.

CONIRAYA
and the Animals

The Inca used this story to explain the different characteristics of some of the animals that lived in their world. They believed the animals had been cursed or blessed by Coniraya (koo nee RAH yah), depending on whether they gave him good or bad news.

A long time ago, after the world had come into being, spirits still wandered Earth. Animals existed, but they were not the animals we know today because they had not been given their different characteristics. One of the Earth spirits, Coniraya, could be quite naughty. He often pretended to be the creator god, Viracocha (vihr uh KOH chuh), and he loved to deceive people. He would dress up as a beggar in rags and mingle among people who had no idea who he really was.

One day, a beautiful woman named Cavillaca (ka vill AH ka) sat weaving beneath a tree. Many men admired her, but she lived alone. When Coniraya saw her, he fell completely in love. He turned himself into a bird and flew into Cavillaca's tree. It was laden with fruit, and when Cavillaca ate a fruit that Coniraya had touched, his child immediately began to grow within her.

Cavillaca gave birth to a boy. On his first birthday, she called all the men in her

village together to find out who her son's father was. Everyone put on their best clothes to meet Cavillaca, but none of them admitted to being her son's father. To try and solve the mystery, Cavillaca put her young son on the floor. She thought that the baby would crawl toward his father.

Coniraya was hiding in the corner, dressed in his rags. When the baby crawled straight to him, Cavillaca could not believe that the scruffy beggar could be the father of her son. Furious, she grabbed the baby and fled. Coniraya put on his smartest clothes, but Cavillaca did not look back. She kept running until she reached the sea. She leaped off a cliff, and she and her son became rocks as they entered the water of the sea.

Coniraya did not know this. He was still looking for them. He met a fox and asked the fox if he had seen Cavillaca. The fox said she was so far away the spirit would never be able to catch her. Coniraya cursed the fox and said that from now on it would have a horrible smell and would be able to go out only at night.

Next, Coniraya met a condor. The condor told him he had seen a woman and that soon Coniraya would catch her. Coniraya thanked the condor and gave it the power to fly away from its enemies. Then he came across a puma. The puma told him the woman was close by. Coniraya blessed him. He said that if anyone killed a puma, they would have to wear its skin, which would make the puma look as if it were still alive. Finally Coniraya met some macaws. They told Coniraya he was too late to catch Cavillaca, so he cursed them. He said that from now on macaws would make loud noises that would make it easy for their enemies to find and catch them.

Coniraya finally arrived at the sea and saw that he was indeed too late. Cavillaca and her son had been turned into rocks. He was so upset that he gathered up the fish from a local goddess's pond and tipped them all into the sea—which is why the sea is full of fish. The goddess was furious and tried to kill Coniraya, but the trickster managed to escape to have more adventures in the future.

The story of Coniraya (koo nee RAH yah) mentions Viracocha (vihr uh KOH chuh), one of the two main Inca creator gods. The Inca believed that Viracocha once walked among the people and instructed them in useful skills. The other main Inca creator god was Pachacamac (pak uh ku MAC). Pachacamac was more of an *oracle* (wise person), whom the Inca consulted when they needed help.

Tiny gold models are a reminder of the importance of llamas to the Inca. Llamas provided transportation, wool for textiles, and meat for eating.

Lanuíla

A Spaniard and an Inca princess appear in fine native clothing after their marriage, in a painting from the early 1700's. Marriage was an important part of Inca society, but the Inca saw marriage as a business arrangement rather than a romantic attachment.

INCA FAMILIES

The Inca lived in extended groups of from 10 to 20 people known as ayullu (eye YOO). A member of an ayullu did not have to be a blood relative in order to belong to the group. The ayullu was hierarchical and very organized: Each person had his or her own position and his or her own tasks. The Inca state made many rules that the ayullu had to follow. The penalties for breaking the rules were harsh.

The Inca believed that the universe was divided into three parts: Hanan Pacha (HA-nahn PAH-cha), the World Above; Hanan Ukhu (HAH nahn OO koo), the World Below; and Kay Pacha (KAY PAH chuh), the Human World. Hanan Pacha contained the sun, moon, and stars and was where the sun god and moon goddess lived. Hanan Ukhu was the world of the spirit.

Lake Titicaca (tee tee KAH kah), high in the Andes Mountains on the border of modern-day Bolivia and Peru, is the largest lake in South America. Different ancient Andean cultures believed its dark blue waters were sacred. The Inca believed that their creator god Viracocha rose from the lake to form the sun, moon, stars, and the first human beings. They thought the sun god, Inti, lived on the Isla del Sol (Island of the Sun) near the Bolivian shore. They also believed that the spirits of the dead returned to the lake.

KONONATOO

and the Hole in the Sky

The Warao (wah row oh) tell this story to explain how they came to live around the delta of the Orinoco River. The story also reminds them that the world is a difficult place.

Kononatoo (koh no ah too), the creator god, lived above the clouds with the first human beings. Down below, Earth was uninhabited. One day, a powerful *shaman* (person with power from the gods), living with other humans above the clouds, shot an arrow into the air. The arrow fell to the floor of the sky, making a hole. When the shaman pulled out the arrow, sand began to slide through the hole, creating a whirlwind and making the hole larger. The hole grew so large that the people above the clouds could peer down through it. They saw Earth with its mountains, its oceans, and its rivers. The people became excited, and some of them decided to go below to see this world.

One of the humans lowered himself from the sky using a rope made from the fiber of the moriche palm. He lowered himself all the way down until he landed on an island at the mouth of a huge river. He explored every bit of the island and then returned to his people above the clouds. He reported, "Earth is amazing. It is surrounded by water. There are lots of fish in the water and lots of birds and lots of moriche to make things with." The other Indians were excited. "We must go and live down there," one of them exclaimed. The elders and great men of the tribes met to make preparations for their descent.

The day came when the Indians had decided they would all move down to Earth. One after another they began to descend down a strong moriche rope they had made especially for the occasion. One human after another slid down the rope.

At last only the shaman who had originally made the hole in the floor of the sky with his arrow was left with his wife. He told his wife to go before him. She was just about to give birth and her stomach was very large. Try as she might, she could not squeeze through the hole. The opening was just too narrow. The shaman tried to help her. He pushed her with his feet and, when that didn't work, he jumped on her. But it was all in vain. She only managed to get one foot, one leg, and one thigh through the gap. There she got stuck forever and became the stars.

When you look at the night sky and see the group of seven stars people call the Great Bear, that is the woman's leg. Her other leg remains wedged in the hole in the sky, closing it forever.

The World of THE WARAO

The Warao (wah row oh) Indians live in the Orinoco (OHR uh NOH koh) Delta of modern-day Venezuela, next to the swampy regions of British Guiana. Because the area is hard to reach, the Warao have had little contact with other Indian tribes or European settlers. In their wetland environment, the most important item the Warao own is their dugout canoes. They serve as floating houses. The Warao travel in them, carry loads in them, and sleep, cook, and eat in them. That's why the Warao are known as the "boat people."

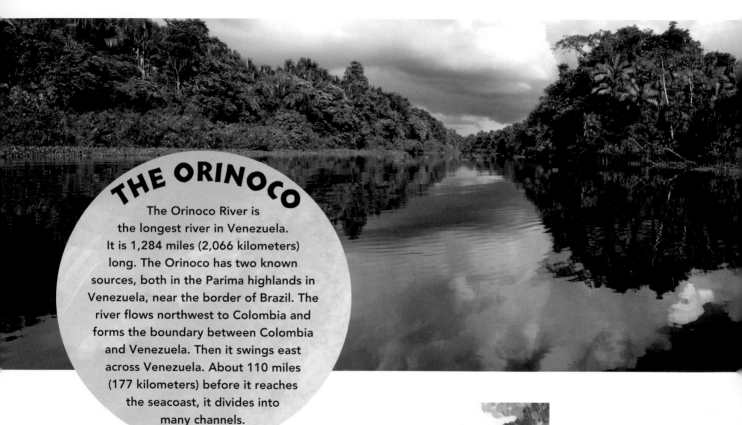

THE ORINOCO

The Orinoco River is the longest river in Venezuela. It is 1,284 miles (2,066 kilometers) long. The Orinoco has two known sources, both in the Parima highlands in Venezuela, near the border of Brazil. The river flows northwest to Colombia and forms the boundary between Colombia and Venezuela. Then it swings east across Venezuela. About 110 miles (177 kilometers) before it reaches the seacoast, it divides into many channels.

The Orinoco Delta has many streams and marshes, so the Warao use canoes to get around. They hollow out tree trunks to make canoes that can hold up to 50 people.

LIFE IN THE SKY

Like the Warao, many other peoples believed that the sky was a world similar to that of Earth, where people lived and animals roamed. Around the world, people identified animal shapes among patterns of stars, called constellations. One of the most easily visible was the Great Bear.

The most important source of food for the Warao is the moriche (mohr ee chee) palm, which they call the "tree of life." The fruit of the moriche palm is high in vitamin C. It is used to make juice, jam, and wine. Even the palm's starchy *pith* (central, spongy tissue) can be used for food. The Warao use all parts of the moriche palm, from the bark to the leaves and the fiber. The fibers are used to make cloth, building materials, and tools. Other important food sources for the Warao include yucca, ocumo (also called taro), bananas, plantains, sugar cane, corn (maize), and rice.

About 20,000 Warao still live in the Orinoco Delta. They live in traditional open-sided huts built from moriche wood. The huts are raised on logs to help avoid the frequent flooding. Palm leaves provide thatch for the roofs.

41

The First Death of

ÁRI AND HIS

RESURRECTION

This story from the Bororo (boh ROH roh) reflects that people's interest in the sky, especially in the sun and the moon. The story also describes the importance—and dangers—of fire.

One day some Indians were fishing. They caught lots of fish and left them cooking on a fire. Méri (MAIR ee), the Sun, and his younger brother Ári (AHR ee), the Moon, came across the fire. They emptied their bodies' water on the fire to put it out and ran off, laughing. The toad saw what they had done. When the Indians returned to their fire, the toad told them who had put it out.

The Indians decided to have their revenge. They gathered together fast-running birds like the emu and partridge. Then they tied glowing coals into the birds' head feathers. The birds found the brothers and ran in a large circle around them. As the coals set fire to the long grass, the brothers climbed into trees to escape. Méri's tree resisted the flames, but Ári's tree burned. All that was left of Ári were some charred bones.

When the fire went out, Méri went to find his brother. He gathered Ári's bones into a pile, but a wolf ate them. Méri challenged the wolf to a race, telling him that tying a belt around his waist would help him run faster. The wolf agreed, so Méri loaned him his belt. Méri pulled the belt tighter and tighter, until the wolf's stomach swelled up. "Now, let's start the race," said Méri, the Sun. The wolf, with his huge belly, soon tripped and fell. He burst into pieces and died.

In the wolf's stomach Méri found a few of Ári's bones, which he arranged in the shape of his brother. For Ári's head, he

used a termite nest, and for his arms and legs he used sticks. Then Méri sprinkled some herbs over the bones, covered them with leaves, and left.

When Méri returned the next day, the termites' nest had turned into a head and the sticks had become arms and legs. To wake Ári, Méri shouted him a warning: "Spirits are coming for you: jaguar, leopard, rattlesnake. Flee quickly." The warning worked. Ári sat up, wide awake. Méri said, "Now that I have called you back to life, let's go hunting again."

The World of THE BORORO

The Bororo (boh ROH roh) live in the heart of Brazil. Their homeland is mainly cerrado, a type of savannah covered by forest or grasslands.

The Bororo people have been severely harmed by their contact with non-Bororo people. Toward the end of the 1800's, prospectors mined gold and diamonds in Bororo territory. They brought with them diseases to which the Bororo had no natural resistance. The Western Bororo were wiped out. Today, only the Eastern Bororo remain, and they number only around 1,500 people.

BORORO MYTHS

Bororo myths often feature the two brothers: Méri (MAIR ee), the Sun, and Ári (AHR ee), the Moon. They are represented as a strong older brother and a weak younger brother. But they are not like the hero brothers of other South American myths. These brothers are tricksters, who can harm people as well as help them, as when they put out the fishers' fire. The brothers are also different from brothers in other myths of the region, because both the sun and the moon are men. In most South American myths, the sun is male and the moon is female. The Bororo do not explain how the brothers came to be, but they have many stories about their adventures.

In most myths, the moon is female. But to the Bororo, the moon is male.

A Bororo woman uses her finger to press a design into the surface of a clay pot she is making.

Today, the Bororo live by hunting animals and birds, gathering plants, and fishing in the region's wetlands. Both fishing and hunting play a part in the stories of Ári and Méri.

VILLAGE COURT

The name *Bororo* means *village court*. The Bororo live in villages consisting of houses arranged in a circle. A special house for men, called the Baito, sits in the center of the village. To the west of the Baito is the village's ceremonial court, called the Bororo. There the villagers hold their most important ceremonies.

KUAT AND THE

The Kamayurá people tell this myth to explain why the day is light and the night is dark, and why the moon waxes and wanes in the sky.

Before the world was created, humans lived in total darkness. The only light belonged to the birds, who lived in a kingdom ruled by the vulture king, Urubutsin (oo ruh BUT sin).

The twins Kuat (KOO hwuht) and Iae (EE ay) wanted to make life better, so they decided to steal daylight from the birds. "How can we convince Urubutsin to give us some light?" Iae asked Kuat. "What do we know about Urubutsin?" "Well," replied Kuat, "We know he is greedy and that juicy maggots are his favorite food." Then Kuat had a brilliant idea.

The twins made a figure in the shape of a rotting corpse and stuffed it full of maggots. Then they sent it to Urubutsin.

The vulture king licked his lips when he saw the offering and devoured the maggots. "I must visit Kuat and Iae and get some more of these maggots, which are the best I have ever eaten," he said.

The twins made another corpse. They filled it with maggots and then climbed inside it. Urubutsin and his courtiers arrived at the village. As he greedily dived for the maggots, Kuat and Iae leaped out and threw a net over him.

The other vultures flew off, leaving Urubutsin a prisoner. He struggled so hard to escape the net that his feathers turned to tatters. He grew hungrier and more depressed until he finally agreed to share the light with the twins, who then released him.

BIRDS

As he flew off, the vulture king tossed a box of light to the brothers, who threw it into the sky. Kuat chose the biggest piece of the light for his home, which he called the Sun. Iae chose a smaller piece, which he called the Moon. Between them, they keep the darkness away. Sometimes Iae gets tired. As he falls asleep, the darkness nibbles away at the light, and the moon grows smaller. But eventually Iae wakes up, and the moon grows larger and brighter in the sky.

The entire Kamayurá tribe lives in one village in Brazil near the Xingu (shing GOO) River.

AT HOME WITH THE KAMAYURÁ

The Kamayurá name means *raised platform to store meat, pans, and pots.* The tribe lives deep in the Amazon rain forest in a village of houses with round roofs covered with sape grass. The houses are dark inside. The village has one house that is used to store flutes, which only the men may play. After a measles epidemic in the 1950's, the Kamayurá were reduced to fewer than 500 people. Today the population is growing again.

A Kamayurá man plays the pipes during a ceremony. The pipes are stored in a special hut and are played only by men.

Around 400 to 500 *indigenous* (native) Indian groups, numbering as many as a million people, live in the Amazon rain forest, the world's largest rain forest. It covers around 2.5 million square miles (6.5 million square kilometers), with 60 percent of it lying in Brazil. Development, *deforestation* (the destruction of forests), disease, and gold mining threaten the cultures of the remaining native peoples of the Amazon rain forest.

The kapok tree towers over many other types of vegetation in the Amazon rain forest. The local peoples use it for many purposes. Its lightweight wood makes it ideal for carving dugout canoes. The silky fibers of the seed pods are used to stuff pillows and mattresses for bedding. Different parts of the tree are also used to make remedies for a number of illnesses.

The Xingu River flows over 1,200 miles (1,930 km) through the rain forest before flowing into the mighty Amazon River. The Kamayurá and other tribes who live along the Xingu River tell stories about the Oi (oy), who were a mythical race of beings from a long time ago. The Oi were very tall people who were said to sing as they went through the rain forest. The Amazonian tribes claim to have been able to hear the Oi singing in the distance until quite recently. Now, however, the Oi have finally fallen silent. But the Kamayurá and their neighbors still sing the Oi chants today.

Stealing Fire from JAGUAR

The Wichí (wee CHEE) Indians of Argentina tell this story to explain the origins of fire. The story reflects the importance many South American peoples attached to the jaguar.

A long time ago, only Jaguar possessed fire. His fire burned all day and all night. Jaguar guarded the fire jealously, but he sometimes gave away a few embers if he received a gift. People needed fire to cook with, so they would regularly bring him fish, and Jaguar would give them the embers they needed to make a fire.

One day, a passing rodent stopped and admired the fire. When Jaguar wasn't looking, the rodent tried to steal some embers. Jaguar saw what he was up to and said, "Don't touch the fire, you will burn yourself." The little animal shivered and pretended he was cold, then he moved closer to the fire again. He picked up an ember and put it under his chin. He said to Jaguar, "Now I feel warm." Then he ran away as fast as he could and threw the ember into the middle of a meadow.

Soon the grass started to burn. Jaguar rushed to the meadow and tried to put out the fire, but he could not. People rushed to the meadow and took all the embers to make their fires. That is how the people of the world got fire.

Now that Jaguar was no longer the only one with fire, no one brought him fish. He lay in his den and grew so hungry he became sick. One day, a small tiger cat came to see him. The cat was an expert hunter. He could see that Jaguar needed help.

The tiger cat went to look for prey to bring to Jaguar. He jumped on a huge bird, but he could not kill it outright—it was too big. The bird tried to fly off with the cat still on its back. They were high off the ground before the cat was able to kill the bird. Both fell to the ground like stones, but the cat landed on its feet and was not injured. He took the bird to Jaguar, who ate it up.

Then the two cats went hunting together. At first, Jaguar was hopeless. He was a fast runner, but he could not hold on to his prey. Then he realized that if he used his claws, he could kill prey quickly. Soon Jaguar became such a good hunter that he was no longer hungry. But because he no longer had any fire to cook his food, he had to eat his meat raw.

The World of **THE WICHÍ**

A Wichí woman weaves a basket from the fibers of a forest plant, the chaguar bromeliad. The Wichí depend on the rich resources of the forest.

THE WICHÍ

The Wichí traditionally lived by fishing and hunting small animals. After meeting Europeans in the early 1600's, they continued to follow their traditional ways of life. Every summer, the modern Wichí move to straw huts built along the banks of area rivers. Using huge nets, families work together to catch fish, which they sell.

Cacti are common in the Gran Chaco.

The Pilcomayo (peel koh MY oh) River (left) is one of several rivers that flow through the Gran Chaco (grahn CHAH koh), where the Wichí live. The Gran Chaco spreads across parts of present-day Argentina, Bolivia, and Paraguay in South America. It is a sparsely populated, hot, semi-arid lowland area. The land is characterized by grasslands and scrub forests. The Gran Chaco was once home to about 35 different tribal groups.

THE CULT OF THE JAGUAR

The cult of the jaguar was popular throughout ancient Central and South America. The cat was the largest and most successful predator in the Americas. Many ancient peoples saw it as a messenger between the physical world and the world of the spirits—an animal equivalent of a shaman. The jaguar was a symbol of strength, athleticism, and magic. People were in awe of its speed and agility. Shamans wore necklaces made of jaguar teeth and clothed themselves in jaguar skins as a sign of their supernatural powers.

The Creation of the
UNIVERSE

The Mapuche (mah POO cheh) of Patagonia tell this myth about the creation of the universe and features of the landscape in which they live. The story also explains the origins of some of the natural dangers the Mapuche face.

The big spirit, Füta Newen (FEW tah NEW en), was all-powerful and controlled everything. He could make anything possible. He lived with a number of little spirits, his children. Some of them—his sons—did not like the big spirit having so much power. They wanted some for themselves. So the sons of the big spirit stopped listening to him and rebelled.

Füta Newen was furious and spat on his sons, turning them into stone. Their bodies were too heavy to stay in the sky, so they fell to Earth, where they became mountains. Some of the rebellious spirits also became trapped inside Earth in the Munche Mapu, an evil place where tormented spirits live. The spirits became angry and turned the mountains into smoking, erupting volcanoes. Other sons became thunder and lightning.

However, not all the little spirits were angry or rebellious. Other spirits stayed loyal to the big spirit. These were the female spirits. They cried and cried at the rebellion of their brothers; their tears spilled out over the mountains and became the rivers and lakes. The soil was formed from a mixture of water (the daughters' tears) and ash (the brothers' anger). As they mourned their brothers, the sisters were turned into stars.

Next the big spirit became Cahu Elchefe (ka WHO el JEF ee), or Elchen (el CHEN), and created humankind. He did this by dividing himself into two: a male sun, which was the husband and father, and a female moon, which was the wife and mother.

Woman was first to be created from a daughter star and was placed on Earth. Her job was to give life. Every plant

animal, and other form of life came from her footsteps. To protect her and to provide food for her, man was created next from a lightning son. The moon and the sun took turns looking after their children; that's why there is a balance between day and night. The sun taught his children how to sow seeds, harvest the plants, and make fire.

The moon taught them about the passing of the seasons and when they should sow their seeds.

But the harmonious world did not last forever. Two forces on Earth wage a constant struggle. Kai-Kai (ky ky), the flood, has the power to kill people and animals with its torrents of water.

Tren-Tren, its rival, is the solid Earth of the soaring mountains and hills. It tries to defeat Kai-Kai by saving humans and animals. When Kai-Kai sends huge floods to drown people, the people are transformed into such water creatures as whales, fish, and even mermaids.

Some humans flee to the top of the mountains to escape the flood, but to survive, they resort to eating one another. This situation disturbs the natural order. When there is only one couple left in the world, the big spirit tells them that, to restore order, they must throw their only child into the raging waters. When the couple carries out the sacrifice, order is re-established. Then the couple can have more children to repopulate the world.

The World of THE MAPUCHE

The Mapuche (mah POO cheh) live in Patagonia, a region near the tip of South America, in the southern parts of Chile and Argentina. The landscape is often mountainous, with many high, snow-covered peaks, including Chile's Towers of Paine (above). Active volcanoes send plumes of smoke into the sky. The weather can be bitterly cold. Great sheets of ice, called glaciers, move slowly down the mountain sides to break off into the sea.

MAPUCHE BELIEFS

The most powerful god in Mapuche mythology is Ngenechén (goo neh CHEHN). Over time, the Mapuche have blended his positive and negative aspects with the Christian God. Ngenechén's main function is to keep order. The Mapuche believe he keeps them well and that they must offer animal sacrifices to keep him happy. Otherwise, they will suffer earthquakes, droughts, and poverty.

A Mapuche chief wears a traditional costume and carries a war spear, in a drawing from the 1850's. Mapuche women were known for the beautiful textiles they wove.

THE MAPUCHE

The Mapuche (their name means *people of the land*) lived in villages in scattered communities across present-day south-central Chile and southwest Argentina. A chief, or cacique (ka SEEK), was the head of the settlement. The Mapuche grew crops and hunted. They were also skilled warriors. The ancient Mapuche once fought against attempts by the Inca of Peru to conquer them. Their modern descendants struggle to maintain their culture.

Mapuche musicians and dancers celebrate the "sunrise of the new sun." This new year's celebration takes place on June 24, the Winter Solstice, just after the shortest day of the year in the Southern Hemisphere. At dawn, everyone bathes in a river or stream to purify themselves for the coming year.

DEITIES OF CENTRAL AND SOUTH AMERICA

Ah Mun (ah muhn)
Also known as Yum Kaax (yoom KAHSH), Ah Mun was the Maya lord of the forests and god of agriculture, who helped bring fertility to the crops and was related to an earlier god of the corn.

Ári (AHR ee), the Moon
A trickster god of the Bororo Indians and younger brother of Méri, the Sun. He helps as well as harms humans.

Coniraya (koo nee RAH yah)
A trickster god of the Inca who gave animals their characteristics.

Füta Newen (FEW tah NEW en)
The big spirit of the Mapuche Indians who created people. His sons rebelled against him.

Heavenly Twins
Hunhun-Ahpu (hoon-hoon-ah-poo) and Vukub-Ahpu (voo-koob-ah-poo), also known as the Divine Twins. The Inca believed that the Heavenly Twins were champion players of the ball game tlachtli, who journeyed to the underworld to play the Twelve Lords of Xibalba (shaw BALH bah), who killed them.

Hero Twins
Hunahpu (hoon ah POO) and Xbalanque (shaw BAHL ahn kay), the sons of Hunhun-Ahpu. They play ball with the Twelve Lords of Xibalba to

avenge the death of their father. They sacrificed themselves to defeat the evil Lords and establish a new world order for humans.

Huracán (hoo rah KAHN)
The name of the Maya god of storms gave us the word *hurricane*. Huracán was important during the gods' attempts to create human beings.

Iae (EE ay)
A god of the Kamayurá Indians who, with his brother Kuat, stole fire from the vulture to give to people; he later became the moon.

Inti
The sun god of the Inca. One of the most powerful of the Inca deities, he was represented by a golden disk surrounded by the rays of the sun. Inti was the divine ancestor of the Inca rulers on earth. His wife was Mama Kilya, the goddess of the moon, who controlled the Inca ritual calendar.

Jaguar
In Central America and northern regions of South America, the fanged cat was sometimes seen as the creator god. In many cultures, Jaguar was a representation of power and strength who was seen as the master of all animals.

Kononatoo (koh noh nuh too)
The Warao of the Orinoco River believed that the creator god, Kononatoo, wanted them to live in the sky and was angry when they found a way to Earth.

Kuat (KOO hwuht)
A god of the Kamayurá Indians who, with his brother Iae, stole fire from the vulture to give to people and who became the sun.

Mama Ocllo (MAH mah oh KLOH)
The Inca believed that Mama Ocllo was the daughter of either Viracocha the creator god or Inti the sun god. She was the sister and wife of Manco Cápac and helped him found the Inca people; she was said to have taught Inca women how to weave cloth.

Manco Capac (MAHN koh KAH pahk)
In Inca myth, Manco Capac was the first ruler of the Inca and the founder of their capital, Cuzco. He was the son of either the creator god Viracocha or Inti, the sun god, who sent him and his brothers and sisters to earth. Manco Capac united the peoples of the Cuzco Valley to create the Inca, whom he ruled with his sister and wife, Mama Ocllo.

Méri (MAIR ee), the Sun
A trickster god of the Bororo Indians and older, stronger brother of Ári, the Moon. He helps as well as harms humans.

Ngenechén (goo neh CHEHN)
The Mapuche of the lower part of South America worship Ngenechén as one of their most important gods and their creator, although he was traditionally seen more as the guiding spirit of the Mapuche people.

Pachacamac (pah chuh KAH mahk)
The ancient peoples who lived on the coast of Peru saw Pachacamac, the "earth-maker," as a creator god. He was later adopted by the Inca.

Pachamama (PAH chuh MAH mah)
For the Inca, Pachamama was the goddess of Earth who received their sacrifices of llamas and other animals.

Urubutsin (oo ruh BUT sin)
Peoples of the Amazon basin believed that the vulture god Urubutsin ruled the kingdom of the birds. Urubutsin jealously kept light from humans until he was captured by Ári and Méri, the gods of the moon and sun, and forced to give up the light.

Viracocha (vihr uh KOH chuh)
The Inca worshiped Viracocha as their ultimate deity, who was god of storms and of the sun. He was said to have emerged from Lake Titicaca to create the universe. After he created humans, he wandered the earth disguised as a beggar to teach people the elements of civilization.

Vucub Caquix (voo KOOB kay KEESH)
The Maya told stories about a ferocious bird god named Vucub Caquix, who, in an age before humans existed, pretended to be the sun and the moon until he was killed by the Hero Twins, Hunahpu and Xbalanque.

GLOSSARY

cacique The name given to a chief by many Latin American peoples.

city-state An independent state formed by a powerful city and the lands over which it has control.

constellation A group of stars that form an identifiable pattern, such as an animal or a mythological figure.

creation The process by which the universe was brought into being at the start of time.

creator In myth, a creator god is one that creates the universe or the earth, geographical features, and often all humans or a particular culture. Creation myths explain the origins of the world, but often do so by describing actions that seem to take place in a world that already exists.

cult A system of religious devotion based on a particular individual or object.

delta A triangular-shaped area of water channels and wetlands where a river enters the sea.

dugout canoe A canoe made by hollowing out a single tree trunk.

hieroglyphic A system of writing that uses picture symbols rather than letters.

irrigate To provide a regular supply of water to an area of land in order to allow crops to grow.

myth A traditional story that a people tell to explain their own origins or the origins of natural and social phenomena. Myths often involve gods, spirits, and other supernatural beings.

ritual A solemn religious ceremony in which a set of actions are performed in a specific order.

sacred Something that is connected with the gods or goddesses that should be treated with respectful worship.

sacrifice An offering made to a god or gods, often in the form of an animal or even a person who is killed for the purpose. Sacrifices also take the shape of valued possessions that might be buried, placed in caves, or thrown into a lake for the gods.

savannah A grassy plain with few trees.

shaman A person who enters a trance during a religious ritual in order to gain access to the world of the spirits; in many cultures, a shaman is seen as an intermediary between humans and the spiritual world.

step pyramid A four-sided structure that rises to a point or flattened point by means of a series of levels, each of which is smaller than the level beneath it.

supernatural Describes something that cannot be explained by science or by the laws of nature, which is therefore said to be caused by beings such as gods, spirits, or ghosts.

terrace One of a series of flat steps dug into a slope in order to provide land for farming.

trickster A supernatural figure who engages in mischievous activities that either benefit or harm humans. The motives behind a trickster's behavior are not always clear. Tricksters appear in various shapes in myths around the world, including Coyote and Raven in Native American cultures and Anansi the spider in West Africa.

FOR FURTHER INFORMATION

Books

Bingham, Ann. *South and Meso-American Mythology A to Z* (Mythology A to Z Series). Facts on File, 2004.

Dalal, Anita. *Mesoamerican Myths* (Myths from Around the World). Gareth Stevens Publishing, 2010.

Harper, Jo. *Birth of the Fifth Sun and Other Mesoamerican Tales.* Texas Tech University Press, 2008.

Hyde, Natalie. *Understanding Mesoamerican Myths* (Myths from Around the World). Crabtree Publishing, 2013.

Jolley, Dan, and David Witt. *The Hero Twins Against the Lords of Death: a Mayan Myth* (Graphic Myths and Legends). Graphic Universe, 2008.

Jones, David. *The Myths and Religion of the Incas: An Illustrated Encyclopedia of the Gods, Myths, and Legends of the First Peoples of South America.* Anness, 2008.

Laughton, Timothy. *Exploring the Life, Myth, and Art of the Maya* (Civilizations of the World). Rosen Publishing Group, 2011.

National Geographic Essential Visual History of World Mythology. National Geographic Society, 2008.

Philip, Neil. *Eyewitness Mythology* (DK Eyewitness Books). DK Publishing, 2011.

Roza, Greg. *Incan Mythology and other Myths of the Andes* (Mythology Around the World). Rosen Central, 2008.

Schomp, Virginia. *The Ancient Maya* (Myths of the World). Marshall Cavendish Benchmark, 2010.

Steele, Paul Richard. *Handbook of Inca Mythology* (Handbooks of World Mythology). ABC-CLIO, 2004.

West, David, et al. *Mesoamerican Myths* (Graphic Mythology). Rosen Publishing Group, 2006.

Websites

http://www.godchecker.com/pantheon/south-american-mythology.php
A directory of South American deities from God Checker, written in a light-hearted style but with accurate information.

http://www.godchecker.com/pantheon/incan-mythology.php
The God Checker index of Incan deities, with links to individual entries.

http://www.pantheon.org/areas/mythology/americas/
Encyclopedia Mythica page with links to many pages about myths from different American cultures.

http://www.mythome.org/SouthAm.html
A page with an exploration of the different cultures of Peru and links to different myths, sorted by theme.

http://www.crystalinks.com/mayancreation.html
This Crystal Links collection has a number of Mayan creation stories.

http://maya.nmai.si.edu/the-maya/creation-story-maya
Smithsonian website that explores the Maya creation story.

http://www.pbs.org/opb/conquistadors/peru/adventure1/a2.htm
A PBS website that includes information on Inca gods and religion.

INDEX

PRONUNCIATION KEY	
Sound	As in
a	hat, map
ah	father, far
ai	care, air
aw	order
aw	all
ay	age, face
ch	child, much
ee	equal, see
ee	machine, city
eh	let, best
ih	it, pin, hymn
k	coat, look
o	hot, rock
oh	open, go
oh	grow, tableau
oo	rule, move, food
ow	house, out
oy	oil, voice
s	say, nice
sh	she, abolition
u	full, put
u	wood
uh	cup, butter
uh	flood
uh	about, ameba
uh	taken, purple
uh	pencil
uh	lemon
uh	circus
uh	labyrinth
uh	curtain
uh	Egyptian
uh	section
uh	fabulous
ur	term, learn, sir, work
y	icon, ice, five
yoo	music
zh	pleasure